DISCOVER WHAT'S INSIDE

KU-350-199

LET'S GET STARTED

What are the most dangerous animals on the planet? Which creatures are terrifying enough to give you nightmares? Which species should you avoid at all costs? On the following pages you can read all about the world's top killer creatures!

Each category includes the top ten animals chosen for...

- 🐾 **their deadly details**
- 🐾 **their killer weapons**
- 🐾 **how they attack their prey or a predator.**

If they're known to cause human deaths, that's been taken into account, too.

> Animals develop killer weapons for two reasons – to hunt or to defend themselves. So, they don't necessarily have to be predators to make the top ten in each category. Some plant-eaters (called "herbivores") still have impressive defence weapons and surprising ways of attacking and killing those who might predate *them* instead – including humans!

Abbreviation chart:

oz = ounces	in = inches	mph = miles per hour
lbs = pounds	ft = foot	gal = gallons

KILLER SCORES

DEADLY DETAILS: 9

KILLER WEAPONS: 10

ATTACK METHOD: 9

KILLER SCORE: 28/30

DEADLY DETAILS

This takes into account the animal's size, camouflage ability and habitat. Also considered is the animal's fear factor – from its terrifying appearance to its legendary deadliness.

KILLER WEAPONS

For this score, marks are awarded to an animal based on the number and length of its teeth or claws, the effects of any toxins it produces or diseases it transmits, any ability to leap or jump, its strength and its speed. Also taken into account are the amount of pain it can cause and any super-senses it has for tracking down prey or avoiding a predator.

ATTACK METHOD

The highest scoring animals all have some of the following criteria in common: high levels of aggression, an element of surprise and efficient attack techniques. Extra points are also awarded for unusual or particularly terrifying methods of attack.

KILLER SCORE

Whatever the overall score, turn the pages with care – because all the animals in this book are extremely dangerous!

KILLER
LAND MAMMALS

Sharp claws, super speed and enormous jaws – you'll find all of these in this list of the top ten killer land mammals. But it might surprise you that some of the most fearsome land mammals aren't necessarily the best hunters. Even those who just eat plants still have terrifying killer weapons for defending themselves from possible attackers, or protecting their territories. So even if meat isn't on the menu, you still might want to keep your distance!

BLACK RHINOCEROS

(Scientific name: Diceros bicornis)

Eats: leafy plants, shoots and fruits.

Living in ever-decreasing numbers in central and eastern Africa, the black rhinoceros is a terrifyingly powerful creature that can trample anything in its path.

DEADLY DETAILS:

Despite its name, the black rhinoceros usually has tough white or grey skin. Their horns, which are used for intimidation and defence, can reach a massive 1.4 metres (4.6 ft) in length and are incredibly strong. But let's not forget the obvious – these guys are huge, and can weigh an incredible 1.4 tonnes (3,086 lbs).

KILLER WEAPONS:

A group of rhinos is known as a "crash" – which is an apt description of these guys. Aside from their enormous horns, their main weapon is the sheer, brute force behind their ability to crash their way through pretty much anything, thundering along at speeds of up to 63 kilometres per hour (39 mph).

ATTACK METHOD:

As herbivores, they don't hunt for prey, but they are still known to instinctively attack pretty much anything in defence of themselves or their young. Their poor eyesight means they rely on their sense of smell and hearing to detect anything they perceive as a threat. You wouldn't want to accidentally cross paths with a black rhino – they use the largest of their two horns as a weapon and can trample or gore their opponents to death.

KILLER SCORES

DEADLY DETAILS: 6
KILLER WEAPONS: 5
ATTACK METHOD: 6
KILLER SCORE: 17/30
BRUTE STRENGTH AND DEADLY FORCE

CAPE BUFFALO

(Scientific name: Syncerus caffer)

Eats: leaves, shrubs and grass.

The animal most feared by hunters and safari guides in Africa, the cape buffalo might be a herbivore, but it still has the instinct to attack and kill other animals.

DEADLY DETAILS:

With large heads and thick horns, the cape buffalo are the beasts of the savannah plains. Due to their black or charcoal-grey hair, they are easy to spot in the grass and usually live in large herds. Buffalos living on their own or in small groups are much more aggressive and unpredictable than those in larger groups, and will attack anything they perceive as a threat.

KILLER WEAPONS:

With an enormous weight of 870 kilograms (1,918 lbs) and four times the strength of an ox, they are a good match for their African wild cat predators. When they charge, they can hit speeds of 56 kilometres per hour (35 mph) and confront their targets with their horns.

ATTACK METHOD:

Cape buffalos chase down other animals head on, and they will also charge without warning at humans or vehicles, circling back on anything that threatens them with a counter-attack. These guys are known for causing a high human death toll from overturning jeeps and trucks to trampling people to death. Most incredibly, a cape buffalo will continue to charge even if shot in the heart.

KILLER SCORES

DEADLY DETAILS: 6

KILLER WEAPONS: 6

ATTACK METHOD: 6

KILLER SCORE: 18/30
THE UNPREDICTABLE HEAVY-WEIGHT OF AFRICA

POLAR BEAR

(Scientific name: Ursus maritimus)

Eats: seals, fish, birds' eggs and marine animal carcasses.

Polar bears live in the Arctic region, where they sit at the very top of the food chain. They're the largest land carnivores in the world and can survive by living off their own fat reserves for months at time, whenever food is scarce.

DEADLY DETAILS:

Uniquely suited to life on the ice, polar bears have thicker fur than any other bear and a huge layer of blubber, providing them with insulation and helping them float in the water. Although their fur appears white, this is just a clever camouflage trick – it's actually transparent and is reflecting the white ice around them.

KILLER WEAPONS:

A polar bear's sense of smell is so strong that it can detect a seal on the ice from as far as 32 kilometres (19 miles) away. It can run at a speed of up to 40 kilometres per hour (24 mph) and has incredibly powerful muscles to help it tackle its prey. That's without even mentioning its sizeable canine teeth and razor-sharp claws...

ATTACK METHOD:

Using its sense of smell, a polar bear will locate a seal's breathing hole in the ice and lay in wait for it to emerge – sometimes for hours or days at a time. When it spots its opportunity, the bear uses its immense speed and muscle power to pounce on the seal and drag it onto the land to feed on it. As excellent swimmers, these bears will also break through the ice to attack seal pups in their dens.

KILLER SCORES

DEADLY DETAILS: 6

KILLER WEAPONS: 6

ATTACK METHOD: 7

KILLER SCORE: 19/30
A GREAT COMBINATION OF SIZE, SPEED AND PATIENCE

SPOTTED HYENA

(Scientific name: Crocuta crocuta)

Eats: birds, snakes and mammals (from antelope and zebras to small elephants).

Found in the open plains of sub-Saharan Africa, the spotted hyena is the largest of all three species of hyena. Although they are both hunters and scavengers, they get up to 75 per cent of their food from their own kills.

7

Did you know?

A group of hyenas can devour a whole zebra carcass in just half an hour!

KILLER SCORES

DEADLY DETAILS: 6

KILLER WEAPONS: 6

ATTACK METHOD: 8

KILLER SCORE: 20/30

EXCELLENT STAMINA AND COORDINATION SKILLS

KILLER FACT

IF A LION FEASTING ON A CARCASS IS OUTNUMBERED BY HYENAS, THE LION WILL GIVE WAY TO THE HYENAS.

DEADLY DETAILS:

Spotted hyenas have muscular necks and powerful shoulders supporting their large heads and short, blunt muzzles. Their coarse, woolly fur is spotted and sandy or greyish-brown in colour, helping them blend in with their grassland environment.

KILLER WEAPONS:

One of the most impressive weapons a hyena has is its stamina – its large heart gives it incredible endurance for relentlessly chasing down prey over long distances. They have powerful jaws, capable of crushing elephant bones, and sharp eyesight and hearing for tracking prey in the dark.

ATTACK METHOD:

Single hyenas will hunt small animals by themselves, but for larger prey like wildebeest and zebras, hyenas hunt in coordinated packs. This gives them a high rate of hunting success. Working together, they isolate the weakest target in a herd and pursue it at speeds of up to 50 kilometres per hour (31 mph). Then they bite their prey until it dies, either of shock or loss of blood.

GRIZZLY (BROWN) BEAR

(Scientific name: Ursos arctos horribilis)

Eats: fish, fruit, insects, large and small mammals.

Grizzly bears have the most unpredictable behaviour of all the brown bears and are found in North America.

DEADLY DETAILS:

Fully grown grizzly bears are around 1 metre (3.3 ft) tall at the shoulder and can weigh as much as 360 kilograms (793 lbs). Though huge, they can still move at speeds of 48 kilometres per hour (29 mph) so you wouldn't fancy your chances of running away from one of these!

KILLER WEAPONS:

Grizzly bears have powerful jaws and teeth, with large canines and incisors. Their sense of smell is 700,000 times stronger than a human's. They have long, thick claws that, though mainly used for digging, come in useful when attacking prey. They are extremely strong and can overpower pretty much any animal found in their natural habitat.

ATTACK METHOD:

Unlike other bears, grizzly bears can't climb trees to escape attackers, so they will stand their ground when they feel threatened. Making growling noises, they will rise up on their back legs to demonstrate their sheer size, before biting and clawing at their opponent.

KILLER SCORES

DEADLY DETAILS: 7

KILLER WEAPONS: 7

ATTACK METHOD: 7

KILLER SCORE: 21/30

ARMED AND DEADLY WHEN PROVOKED

LEOPARD

(Scientific name: Panthera pardus)

Eats: reptiles, fish and mammals
(ranging from porcupines to wildebeest).

KILLER SCORES

DEADLY DETAILS: 7

KILLER WEAPONS: 7

ATTACK METHOD: 9

KILLER SCORE: 23/30

WITH EXTRA POINTS FOR STEALTH

5

Despite being the most common of Africa and Asia's big cat species, leopards are also the most elusive. They are cunning creatures who have been known to develop a taste for human flesh.

DEADLY DETAILS:

Most leopards have light fur with dark spots, or "rosettes", which help them blend in with their environment not only on the ground but also up in the trees. They are efficient climbers and can leap across distances of 6 metres (20 ft). Not only is the leopard one of the strongest mammals on Earth, but its stealth-like approach to hunting and its ability to reach a sprinting speed of 60 kilometres per hour (37 mph) means there is little chance of escape...

KILLER WEAPONS:

Leopards have the most powerful bite of any of the big cats – allowing them to target prey as big as gorillas. If not fatal at first, their bites often result in bacterial infections. With curved claws that extend to sharp points and broad paws, they are able to kill small animals with just a single swipe.

ATTACK METHOD:

Mainly hunting at night, leopards first stalk their prey for up to a few hundred metres, cleverly using the camouflage around them, until they get within close enough range. At the optimal time, they pounce and swipe at their target with their claws and direct a skull-crushing killing bite to the head or throat. They can also lie in wait in trees to ambush their prey from above.

BENGAL TIGER

(Scientific name: Panthera tigris tigris)

Eats: large mammals such as deer, antelope and buffalo, and also birds.

The Bengal tiger is one of the fastest animals in the world. Found mainly in India and some other parts of Asia, they often live in close proximity to humans and are on the list of the world's most endangered species.

DEADLY DETAILS:

No two Bengal tigers have the same pattern of black stripes on their orange bodies, which help them blend in with their forest and grassland environments. Their back legs are longer than their front, with robust muscles to help them jump and pounce, and their large, padded feet allow them to sneak up on their prey.

KILLER WEAPONS:

With 30 sharp teeth, they have powerful jaws to accompany their long, strong claws, which are perfectly designed for clutching and tearing at their prey. Males can weigh up to 363 kilograms (800 lbs) – the equivalent to 4.5 adult humans – and reach speeds of 65 kilometres per hour (40 mph) when sprinting.

ATTACK METHOD:

Bengal tigers are solitary hunters, who mainly stalk their food at night. From a standstill or mid-run, they leap onto their prey and use their claws to drag it to the ground, before biting at its throat or head.

KILLER FACT

A TIGER'S EYESIGHT IS SIX TIMES BETTER THAN A HUMAN'S. SO THEY WILL SPOT YOU BEFORE YOU SPOT THEM!

Did you know?

A tiger's roar can be heard from a whole 3 kilometres (1.85 miles) away.

KILLER SCORES

DEADLY DETAILS: 8

KILLER WEAPONS: 9

ATTACK METHOD: 8

KILLER SCORE: 25/30

STEALTH AND STRENGTH MAKES
A WINNING COMBINATION

AFRICAN ELEPHANT

(Scientific name: Loxodonta africana)

Eats: vegetation such as grass, bushes, fruit, twigs and roots.

KILLER SCORES

DEADLY DETAILS: 9

KILLER WEAPONS: 9

ATTACK METHOD: 8

KILLER SCORE: 26/30

TERRIFYINGLY INTELLIGENT

3

African elephants are the largest herbivores in the world and, armed with their high intelligence, this makes them truly terrifying killer creatures.

DEADLY DETAILS:

An elephant uses its trunk not only as a tool for digging, finding food or drinking water but also for tearing down trees and fighting. Their ears are used for regulating their body temperature and to signal alarm or anger. An elephant's sharp tusks are actually elongated incisor teeth.

KILLER WEAPONS:

An elephant's most obvious weapon is its gigantic size. The heaviest land mammals on Earth, they are around 4 metres (13 ft) tall and weigh 6 tonnes (13,000 lbs). Their killer tusks can be used to gore victims to death... But perhaps their most terrifying weapon is their superior intelligence. They have complex social structures and excellent memories, which means they can attack purely for revenge. They're thought to kill hundreds of humans every year.

ATTACK METHOD:

When agitated, male elephants have been known to flip safari jeeps over, snap trees in half and have confrontations with black rhinos. Even though they don't hunt prey for food, their strength, size and intelligence means that when they do attack, they can be lethal.

LION

(Scientific name: Panthera leo)

Eats: large mammals like zebras, impalas and wildebeest.

The lion is Africa's top predator, using efficient team-work to maximise its chances of a successful hunt.

DEADLY DETAILS:

A fully grown lion can weigh between 150 kilograms (330 lbs) and 250 kilograms (550 lbs) – just a little smaller than a tiger. Male lions are the only big cats with distinctive manes of fur, which makes them appear larger and more intimidating to other animals. They live in groups of 10–15 individuals, called "prides". The males will patrol the territory while the females do most of the hunting.

KILLER WEAPONS:

With 30 sharp teeth in their vice-like jaws, and five claws on each paw, lions are well-equipped for bringing down large prey. Though not particularly efficient runners, they can still reach 55 kilometres per hour (34 mph) over short distances. Their night vision is six times more powerful than a human's, allowing them to spot their prey in the dark.

KILLER SCORES

DEADLY DETAILS: 8

KILLER WEAPONS: 9

ATTACK METHOD: 10

KILLER SCORE: 27/30
A COORDINATED KILLER
WITH POUNCE POWER

ATTACK METHOD:

Lions are the only cats that work as a team to hunt. Coordinating themselves around a herd of animals, they signal to each other with a cough-like sound to drive the prey into an ambush. Several victims are brought down at once to save the lions from a long, tiring hunt. A lion will also hide patiently before surprising its victim from behind with a quick, deadly pounce.

HIPPOPOTAMUS

(Scientific name: Hippopotamus amphibius)

Eats: grass, fruit and other vegetation.

Hippos are some of the most aggressive creatures in the world. Living in the forests and rivers of Africa, they are unpredictable and territorial mammals.

DEADLY DETAILS:

Hippos live both in the water and on riverbanks and can grow to 5 metres (16 ft) long, weighing as much as two pick-up trucks (3.5 tonnes (7,710 lbs)). Being well-adapted to the water, with eyes, ears and nostrils on the tops of their heads, they can stay submerged for up to five minutes before surprising their victims – catching both humans and other animals off-guard.

Did you know?

Hippos don't technically swim in water – they sink. They run along the bottom of the river to move around.

KILLER WEAPONS:

Hippos are deadly both in and out of the water. They can open their mouths to 180 degrees and the force of one single bite is greater than that of any tiger, gorilla, lion or bear. Hippos are strong enough to crush a crocodile or to break a boat in two. They have long, sharp teeth and canines that resemble tusks, which reach 50 centimetres (20 in) in length.

HIPPOS ARE RESPONSIBLE FOR MORE HUMAN DEATHS ON THE AFRICAN CONTINENT THAN ANY OTHER MAMMAL.

ATTACK METHOD:

Males usually attack to defend their territories, while females attack to protect their young. Hippos are often covered in scars from daily fights with other animals and have been known to tip boats over and attack the crew. Even on land, anything that gets between a hippo and its water faces a creature weighing 3.5 tonnes (7,719 lbs) charging at 48 kilometres per hour (29 mph)!

KILLER SCORES

DEADLY DETAILS: 9

KILLER WEAPONS: 10

ATTACK METHOD: 9

KILLER SCORE: 28/30
THE MOST UNPREDICTABLE, AGGRESSIVE AND TERRITORIAL MAMMAL ON THE LIST!

SPOT THE DIFFERENCE

Can you spot the FIVE differences between these pictures?

H	C	F	O	G	I	N	C	I	S	O	R
N	U	K	A	D	L	W	Z	Y	N	D	L
L	H	N	B	E	A	R	I	D	C	Z	W
A	X	T	B	V	C	L	A	W	S	A	O
M	T	B	D	P	L	U	C	S	M	E	R
F	G	T	B	W	M	L	L	T	R	N	G
T	O	R	A	L	G	U	E	X	I	I	C
Z	F	F	I	C	I	N	S	I	S	N	R
U	P	E	H	Z	K	C	U	C	A	A	V
U	S	C	Y	F	Z	U	Y	J	L	C	O
K	K	B	Z	K	F	L	Y	L	D	E	Y
B	W	E	Q	M	E	Y	Y	M	M	X	G

Answers on page 92

Can you find these words hidden in the grid above?

GRIZZLY • BEAR • CLAWS • ATTACK

MUSCLE • GROWL • INCISOR • CANINE

21

WHICH WORDS WHERE?

Can you fit these words into the spaces?
The first two have been done for you.

CLAWS   SPEED   POWER   ATTACK

~~HUNT~~   STEALTH   ~~TERRITORY~~

T E R R I T O R Y

H
U
N
T

TRUE OR FALSE?

Can you guess whether the statements below are true or false?

	TRUE	FALSE
1. Lions live in the jungle.		
2. Tigers are bigger than lions.		
3. Grizzly bears eat honey.		
4. Hippos only have 16 teeth.		
5. Polar bears hibernate in winter.		
6. Female spotted hyenas are dominant over the males.		
7. Leopards are strong swimmers.		
8. Elephants are scared of mice.		

Answers on page 92

KILLER
SEA CREATURES

Life in the sea has existed for 3 billion years longer than life on land. It's a mysterious place, with much of the oceans yet to be properly explored by humans. It's also a dangerous place – some of the most efficient predators and terrifying creatures lurk in the depths of the seas...

FIRE CORAL

(Scientific name: Millepora spp.)

Eats: plankton.

10

Fire corals might look innocent, but they get their name from the painful sting they give to those who touch them. They're found in the Indian, Pacific and Atlantic oceans and are much feared by divers and snorkellers.

DEADLY DETAILS:

Fire corals are brownish-green, cream or orange, with white tentacle tips. They can have lacy branch-like shapes or look like crusts covering a reef. They're adorned with tiny hairs that are armed with "nematocysts" – which carry a toxin to sting and capture prey.

KILLER WEAPONS:

The fire coral's only defence and hunting weapon is its toxin, but it's a strong one! If a human is stung by fire coral, it feels like an incredibly painful burn that lasts between two days and two whole weeks, sometimes causing vomiting. Their skeletons are also sharp and can scrape the skin.

ATTACK METHOD:

If touched, the nematocysts in the fire coral shoot out little barbed threads full of toxin, just like tiny harpoons. Once stung, the prey is brought inwards by the fire coral's tentacles to be engulfed and digested.

KILLER SCORES

DEADLY DETAILS: 3
KILLER WEAPONS: 7
ATTACK METHOD: 6
KILLER SCORE: 16/30
ONE FLAMING-HOT CREATURE

ELECTRIC EEL

(*Scientific name: Electrophorus electricus*)

Eats: fish, frogs, birds and small mammals.

Despite its name, the electric eel is not an eel at all. It's a type of fish that lives in the murky waters of the Orinoco and Amazon river basins.

DEADLY DETAILS:

These fish can grow to a length of 2.5 metres (8 ft) and have flattened heads and cylinder-like bodies. They get their name from the special cells in their bodies that store power in a similar way to a battery, which can release an enormous electric shock.

KILLER WEAPONS:

Electric eels are speedy, accurate predators, and their main weapon is the electric shock they use to stun or kill their prey. They can generate a 500-watt shock and have been known to knock a horse off its feet! Multiple shocks to a human could cause heart failure and people have drowned in shallow water after a jolt from one of these...

ATTACK METHOD:

The electricity electric eels emit is not only powerful enough to shock or kill, but is used like a radar system in muddy waters to track down prey. Once they've got hold of their prey, they curl around it, holding it between their head and tail. This doubles the strength of the shock and causes contractions in the prey's body until its muscles tire. Then all that's left is to eat it.

KILLER SCORES

DEADLY DETAILS: 5

KILLER WEAPONS: 6

ATTACK METHOD: 7

KILLER SCORE: 18/30
A SHOCKINGLY EFFECTIVE PREDATOR

TEXTILE
CONE SNAIL

(Scientific name: Conus textile)

Eats: fish and molluscs.

8

Textile cone snails live in oceans such as the ones surrounding Australia and French Polynesia. They might look pretty, but don't be fooled by the patterned shells.

DEADLY DETAILS:

At just 9–10 centimetres (3 in) these snails would be easy to miss on the ocean floor. Their shells are decorated in yellow-brown patterns and are shaped roughly like an ice-cream cone.

KILLER WEAPONS:

To catch fast-swimming fish, these snails have developed little harpoons of toxins to fire quickly in any direction. They're sharp enough to get through gloves and wetsuits and the toxins are deadly – one drop is enough to kill more than 20 humans. Symptoms include pain, paralysis, breathing failure and death. And there is no anti-venom...

ATTACK METHOD:

Of course the main point of the cone snail's toxins isn't to kill humans but to catch its food. First, the snail rapidly launches its harpoon at its prey. The fish is instantly paralysed by the venom and the snail draws the entire thing back into its mouth to devour it. Simple – but deadly.

STINGRAY

(Scientific name: Myliobatoidei spp.)

Eats: clams, sea worms and small fish.

Stingrays can be found in shallow waters all around the world and are famous for the deadly sting of their tails.

DEADLY DETAILS:

Stingrays spend most of their time buried in sand or skimming the ocean floor, where their camouflage offers them the best protection from predators. They can grow to almost 2 metres (6 ft) in size and have flattened bodies with long tails.

KILLER WEAPONS:

Stingrays have small, flat teeth that are strong enough to crush mussels and clams.
But the most famous stingray weapon is its tail – which is used mainly for defence. Stingrays have venomous barbs on their tails, which they use to sting anything that threatens them, including humans. The sting can cause excruciating pain, infection from the wound and sometimes death.

KILLER SCORES

DEADLY DETAILS: 5
KILLER WEAPONS: 8
ATTACK METHOD: 6
KILLER SCORE: 19/30
FAMOUSLY DEADLY

ATTACK METHOD:

Stingrays don't use their killer tails to catch prey – they use their mouths. Stingrays' eyes are located at the tops of their heads, so they have little electrical sensors around their mouths to help them sense where their prey is. They then crush it with their teeth and gobble it up.

RED-BELLIED PIRANHA

(Scientific name: Pygocentrus nattereri)

Eats: anything – but especially fish, insects and the carcasses of small mammals.

Found widely throughout South American rivers, these killer creatures are deadly from the second they hatch from their eggs.

DEADLY DETAILS:

Measuring between 14–43 centimetres (5–17 in), these piranhas get their name from the red tinges to their bellies. They have a frightening reputation due to their speed and their insatiable appetites for flesh. They're not predators but scavengers – searching for any food they can find to feast on. They have even been known to eat their own young.

KILLER WEAPONS:

Piranhas are famed for their super-sharp teeth, which are shaped like blades for cutting through meat. They are even used by some communities in South America as weapons. These interlocking teeth are excellent for biting with an incredible force.

ATTACK METHOD:

Piranhas are so ferocious when they attack that they can strip an animal of its flesh in minutes. Weak cattle that venture to drink from piranha-infested waters have been known to be grabbed and completely consumed. When a school of piranhas are feeding, the water around them may fill with blood and look as if it's boiling. They will even take bites out of each other in their eagerness for food.

ORCA

(Scientific name: Orcinus orca)

Eats: sea birds, rays, fish and seals.

5

Orcas, also known as killer whales, live throughout the oceans of the world, but are mostly found in Antarctica and off the coasts of North America, Norway and Iceland.

KILLER SCORES

DEADLY DETAILS: 6

KILLER WEAPONS: 8

ATTACK METHOD: 10

KILLER SCORE: 24/30

CLEVER, COORDINATED TEAMWORK!

KILLER FACT

ORCAS SOMETIMES BREACH THE SURFACE OF THE WATER OR HURL THEMSELVES ONTO ICE SHEETS TO GRAB SEA LIONS AND SEALS. THEY ALSO CREATE WAVES WITH THEIR BODIES TO TIP OVER ICE FLOES SO THAT THEY CAN GOBBLE UP ANY PREY SITTING ON TOP.

DEADLY DETAILS:

These distinctive animals, with their black backs, white bellies and eye patches, can grow to a huge 9.5 metres (31 ft) in length and over 5 tonnes (11,000 lbs) in weight – that's 60 times as heavy as a grown man.

KILLER WEAPONS:

They have excellent eyesight, larger brains than humans and are among the most intelligent animals on Earth. This means they've developed sophisticated hunting methods allowing them to take down animals as big as great white sharks and blue whales – which can be three times the size of the orcas!

ATTACK METHOD:

Orcas hunt in groups, called "pods". To track down their prey they use "echolocation" – making a series of clicking sounds and listening for the echo, to work out how far away a creature is. Then they circle it and force it into a smaller and smaller space by confusing it with bubbles, before taking it in turns to bite and ram into it.

GREAT WHITE SHARK

(Scientific name: Carcharodon carcharias)   Eats: fish, sea lions, seals and whales.

The Great white shark is the largest predatory fish. They live in coastal waters with temperatures between 12–24°C / 54–75°F.

KILLER SCORES

DEADLY DETAILS: 9

KILLER WEAPONS: 8

ATTACK METHOD: 8

KILLER SCORE: 25/30

POWERFUL JAWS WITH BITE

Did you know?

Sharks don't chew their food – they tear off chunks of meat and swallow them whole.

DEADLY DETAILS:

Great white sharks measure around 4.5 metres (15 ft) in length and can be as huge as 6 metres (19 ft) long. They can weigh up to around 2,250 kilograms (4,960 lbs).

KILLER WEAPONS:

With wide jaws and the ability to track down wounded prey from very far away, these are top-notch predators. They have such a strong sense of smell that they would be able to detect just one drop of blood in 100 litres (22 gal) of water! Their 300 triangular teeth are designed to slice instead of grip – a single bite can be fatal.

ATTACK METHOD:

When they spot their prey, great white sharks use the element of surprise to sneak up on it... With their powerful tails, they propel themselves forwards at speeds of up to 24 kilometres per hour (14 mph) – so fast that they can even soar out of the water like whales. They attack with a twisting lunge and tear the flesh from their victims to disable them. Sometimes, they will wait until their prey dies of blood loss before returning to feast on the remains.

KILLER FACT

GREAT WHITE SHARKS ARE HUNTERS STRAIGHT FROM BIRTH. AS SOON AS THEY'RE BORN, THE PUPS SWIM AWAY FROM THEIR MOTHERS AND BEGIN PROWLING THE WATER FOR THEIR OWN FOOD.

STONEFISH

(Scientific name: Synanceia spp.)

Eats: fish and crustaceans.

3

Reef stonefish live in the shallow waters of the Pacific and Indian oceans, including the Great Barrier Reef.

DEADLY DETAILS:

These fish are ugly! But their ugliness also makes for some incredible camouflage against rocks and reefs. Around 40 centimetres (15 in) in size, they resemble stones – hence the name.

KILLER WEAPONS:

These fish are the most venomous fish in the world. They have 13 spines that release venom, usually when any form of pressure is applied to them – so watch where you step! However, this is not what they use to catch prey. Instead, they use their incredible, unpredictable speed to catch their dinner unawares.

KILLER SCORES

DEADLY DETAILS: 9

KILLER WEAPONS: 8

ATTACK METHOD: 8

KILLER SCORE: 25/30

YOU WOULDN'T WANT TO STEP ON ONE OF THESE!

ATTACK METHOD:

Normally, when moving around, stonefish swim very slowly. But when they see a small fish swim past, they lunge for it with amazing speed. A whole attack can last just 0.015 seconds – difficult to see with the human eye. If attacked themselves, stonefish stay where they are and extend their spines to inject venom into their attacker – causing pain, weakness, paralysis and even death.

BLUE-RINGED OCTOPUS

(Scientific name: Hapalochlaena maculosa)

Eats: small crabs and shrimp.

2

KILLER SCORES

DEADLY DETAILS: 8

KILLER WEAPONS: 9

ATTACK METHOD: 9

KILLER SCORE: 26/30

SMALL BUT DEFINITELY DEADLY!

Lurking in the Pacific Ocean, these animals are named after the bright blue rings that show up on their tentacles when they're alarmed.

DEADLY DETAILS:

The blue-ringed octopus is only the size of a golf ball, making it tiny in comparison to the pain it can inflict. They are grey with brown patches, which helps them conceal themselves in rock crevices and shallow pools.

KILLER WEAPONS:

These creatures are intelligent and deceptively strong, with good eyesight. The blue rings that show up on the octopus's legs are a warning to predators not to come any closer. If they do, the octopus has another weapon – a venomous bite that is 1,000 times more powerful than the poison cyanide. The bite itself can be painless, but that makes it even more deadly – a victim who doesn't know they have been bitten also doesn't know to seek help...

ATTACK METHOD:

The octopus pounces on its prey to trap it with its arms and bites it, releasing venom into the wound to paralyse it for easy eating. It's believed they can also dribble the venom into the water around the prey and wait patiently for it to take effect.

Did you know?

A single box jellyfish has enough venom to kill around 50 humans.

KILLER FACT

HUNDREDS OF HUMANS ARE STUNG BY THESE JELLYFISH EVERY YEAR.

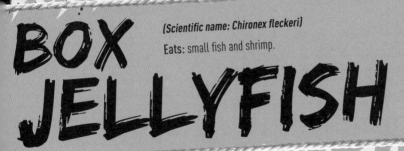

BOX JELLYFISH

(*Scientific name: Chironex fleckeri*)

Eats: small fish and shrimp.

Living around Australia, the Philippines and Malaysia, the box jellyfish is at the top of our list with good reason: it's considered the most venomous animal in the world...

DEADLY DETAILS:

One of the most terrifying things about these creatures is that they're nearly invisible! They have box-shaped, bodies with stinging tentacles 3 metres (9 ft) long. Luckily, the deadly venom in the tentacles reflect sunlight, so you might just be able to see a glimmer of them coming in your direction...

KILLER WEAPONS:

Every one of the box jellyfish's tentacles has around 5,000 stinging cells that are triggered by chemicals or by touch. If a human is stung by one of these, they will go into shock from the pain or die from heart failure or drowning. The pain is so strong that survivors can still feel it for weeks afterwards.

KILLER SCORES

DEADLY DETAILS: 10

KILLER WEAPONS: 10

ATTACK METHOD: 9

KILLER SCORE: 29/30

A THREAT THAT IS HARD TO SEE COMING...

ATTACK METHOD:

Though deadly to humans, the main purpose of the box jellyfish's tentacles is to immobilise fish, so that they're easy enough to gobble up. When hunting, the jellyfishes stretch out their tentacles and twitch them to lure fish towards them, before paralysing them with their stingers.

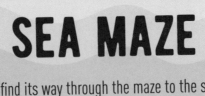

SEA MAZE

Help the fish find its way through the maze to the safety of the reef.

TRUE OR FALSE?

Can you guess whether the statements below are true or false?

	TRUE	FALSE
1. Electric eels can leap from the water to attack prey.		
2. A box jellyfish's tentacles can stay attached to its victim and keep stinging, even after the jellyfish has escaped.		
3. A stonefish can survive for 24 hours out of water.		
4. Piranhas are deadly predators.		
5. A great white shark mother may eat her babies if they stay around too long.		
6. A box jellyfish can lay as many as 100,000 eggs in a single day.		
7. Orcas sleep with one eye open.		
8. Red-bellied piranhas don't have a very good sense of smell.		

Answers on page 93

CROSSWORD

Read the previous chapter, then use the clues to complete the crossword!

CLUES

Across

3. Stingrays use one of these to defend themselves.

4. Stingrays hide beneath this on the sea floor.

5. Piranhas are dangerous as soon as they hatch from their_____.

6. The venomous part of a stonefish.

7. The name of a group of orcas.

Down

1. A blue-ringed octopus's venom is 1,000 times more powerful than this.

2. Orcas blow _____ to confuse their prey.

4. Box jellyfish eat these as well as fish.

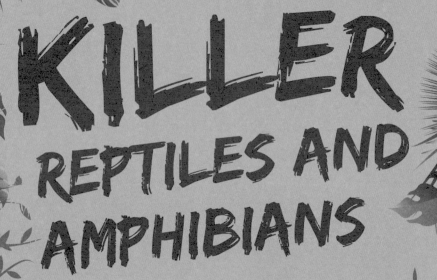

KILLER
REPTILES AND
AMPHIBIANS

Reptiles and amphibians have been on Earth since the time of the dinosaurs, so they've had millions of years to develop the dangerous weapons they use to survive. It's probably no surprise that snakes are included in this list, but there are also certain lizards, turtles and frogs that make the top ten.

GILA MONSTER

(Scientific name: *Heloderma suspectum*)
Eats: small mammals, birds and eggs.

10

Named after the Gila River Basin in the US, the Gila monster has a fearsome reputation, which is why it makes it into the top ten.

DEADLY DETAILS:

The largest lizards in the US, Gila monsters have big heads and muscular jaws, and grow to around 60 centimetres (24 in) long. Although they are called "monsters" they are actually very sluggish animals.

KILLER WEAPONS:

They don't have fangs like snakes but instead have short teeth that are all venomous – supplied by neurotoxins (poison) in their lower jaws. They have a strong bite which allows them to hold on to their prey, chewing until the venom seeps into the wound. Although not fatal to a healthy human, their bite is extremely painful and difficult to break free from.

KILLER SCORES

DEADLY DETAILS: 5

KILLER WEAPONS: 4

ATTACK METHOD: 6

KILLER SCORE: 15/30
A MONSTROUS REPUTATION AND A RELENTLESS BITE

ATTACK METHOD:

Gila monsters only move quickly when they bite and sometimes flip their whole bodies over to help the venom flow into the wound. Prey are either crushed to death by the bites or eaten alive, helped along by contracting muscles in the Gila monster's neck.

NILE MONITOR LIZARD

(Scientific name: *Varanus niloticus*)

Eats: small insects, like ants and termites.

The Nile monitor lizard lives in sub-Saharan Africa and along the River Nile. Ferocious enough to prey on young crocodiles, this lizard isn't fussy – it will eat just about anything it can overpower...

DEADLY DETAILS:

These lizards are the largest in Africa, reaching up to 2.1 metres (6 ft) in length. They have snake-like heads, sharp claws and a powerful tail that acts like a rudder in the water. Their speckled yellow-brown bodies help them keep camouflaged from predators both on land and in the water.

KILLER WEAPONS:

They're fast, with aggressive personalities and a tail that whips with enough force to break a human hand. They boast sharp claws for grabbing and ripping apart their prey and their small yet sharp teeth can crush bones. Their bites are also poisonous – containing some of the same poison found in rattlesnake venom.

KILLER FACT

THESE LIZARDS HAVE BECOME PESTS IN FLORIDA, UNITED STATES, WHERE THEY ARE KNOWN TO ATTACK AND EAT HOUSEHOLD PETS.

ATTACK METHOD:

When threatened, these lizards puff themselves up to pretend they are larger and make hissing sounds. When they lunge at their attackers, they are relentless, using their sharp teeth, claws and powerful tails to bite, whip and tear at their opponents.

KILLER SCORES

DEADLY DETAILS: 5

KILLER WEAPONS: 6

ATTACK METHOD: 6

KILLER SCORE: 17/30

A POWERFUL OPPORTUNISTIC HUNTER

Did you know?

Nile monitor lizards lay up to 60 eggs at a time.

MATA MATA TURTLE

(Scientific name: Chelus fimbriatus)

Eats: frogs, insects,
small mammals and birds.

The next two places in the countdown go to turtles. They might seem to be slow, peaceful creatures at first glance, but they can actually pack a big punch! First up is the bizarre-looking mata mata turtle of the South American river basins.

DEADLY DETAILS:

The mata mata turtle looks like a thing of nightmares. A large, flat turtle, it has a wide mouth and a long snout. Its head resembles fallen leaves while its shell looks like the bark of a tree – so full marks for camouflage! Mata mata turtles only reach 15 kilograms (33 lbs) in weight and 45 centimetres (18 in) in length.

KILLER WEAPONS:

Though they have poor vision, these turtles have a range of senses. Flaps on the side of their heads detect even the slightest hint of movement, allowing them to lash out quickly at their prey. They are able to open their mouths at such speeds that they create a vacuum of water that sucks in the prey whole.

KILLER SCORES

DEADLY DETAILS: 8

KILLER WEAPONS: 6

ATTACK METHOD: 4

KILLER SCORE: 18/30
HIGH MARKS FOR A NIGHTMARISH
APPEARANCE!

ATTACK METHOD:

They prefer to lie at the bottom of shallow rivers and wait for their prey to come to them. When a fish swims by, the turtle thrusts its head forward and sucks the fish into its mouth, expelling the water and swallowing the fish whole. They have also been known to lash out at people and passing boats.

ALLIGATOR SNAPPING TURTLE

(Scientific name: *Macrochelys temminckii*)

Eats: plants, fish, frogs and molluscs.

KILLER SCORES

DEADLY DETAILS: 6

KILLER WEAPONS: 7

ATTACK METHOD: 6

KILLER SCORE: 19/30

POWERFUL JAWS OF STEEL

Found in the waters of the south-eastern United States, these aggressive, prehistoric-looking turtles are among the largest on Earth and are known as the "dinosaurs" of the turtle world.

DEADLY DETAILS:

They have large heads, short snouts and hooked jaws, and the largest are thought to reach an impressive 100 kilograms (220 lbs). Despite their size, when they're covered in algae at the bottom of the water, they have been known to be mistaken for rocks...

KILLER WEAPONS:

By far the most impressive weapon the snapping turtle has is its powerful jaws. Though usually gentle giants, you would do best to steer clear. If disturbed, they can lash out with bone-shattering bites. They also have thick claws on their legs, which they use to tear apart their food.

ATTACK METHOD:

The inside of these turtles' mouths are well camouflaged, and their most impressive, clever way of catching prey is to use a worm-shaped appendage in their mouths to draw curious fish inside. However, when taken by surprise, these turtles enter attack mode. They rise up on their legs, hiss with their mouths open and snap their jaws aggressively in defence.

BEAKED SEA SNAKE

(Scientific name: *Enhydrina schistosa*)

Eats: catfish, pufferfish, other fish or squid.

KILLER SCORES

DEADLY DETAILS: 7

KILLER WEAPONS: 8

ATTACK METHOD: 8

KILLER SCORE: 23/30

AGGRESSIVE AND BAD-TEMPERED
WITH DEADLY VENOM TO BOOT

The beaked sea snake lives in the waters of northern Australia and the Philippines, and is one of the most dangerous and aggressive of the world's snakes.

KILLER FACT

ONE FULL DOSE OF A BEAKED SEA SNAKE'S VENOM CAN KILL 22 PEOPLE.

DEADLY DETAILS:

Reaching lengths of 1.2 metres (3.9 ft), these snakes have flat tails for swimming and nostrils which can close under water. Their front nostrils give them their beak-like appearance and they can stay under water for five hours at a time.

KILLER WEAPONS:

Beaked sea snakes have a reputation for being much more aggressive than other sea snakes. They have shorter fangs than land snakes but they're just as sharp and as deadly. Their quick-acting venom stops their prey from breathing and just a tiny amount (1.5 milligrams (< 0.01 oz)) is enough to kill a human.

ATTACK METHOD:

They hunt down their prey by movement rather than vision, allowing them to dwell in murky waters, out of sight. When prey is detected, the snake lashes forward to inject its venom. When the prey stops struggling, the snake gobbles it down in one go, head first. Its jaws can stretch to allow it to swallow prey twice the size of its neck.

Did you know?

The beaked sea snake is responsible for 90 per cent of all sea snake bites.

KOMODO DRAGON

(Scientific name: Varanus komodoensis)

Eats: meat, including water buffalo, deer, pigs and smaller dragons.

5

At the top of the food chain in the forested lowlands and coasts of Indonesia, the Komodo dragons threaten every living creature in their environment.

DEADLY DETAILS:

Growing to 3 metres (9 ft) long and weighing over 100 kilograms (220 lbs), these beasts are the largest lizards on Earth. They have muscular legs, sharp claws, forked tongues ... and foul breath!

KILLER WEAPONS:

The Komodo dragon's biggest weapon is the venom it secretes from its painful bite. Its 60 serrated teeth create deep wounds to help the venom sink into its victims, causing their blood pressure to drop and sending them into a state of shock. Komodo dragons have flexible skulls to allow them to gulp down large chunks of flesh and powerful tails that can with one swipe knock a water buffalo weighing 500 kilograms (1,100 lbs) off its feet.

ATTACK METHOD:

It charges at large prey, such as pigs, deer and water buffalo, to knock them down, then bites off big chunks of flesh. Once it gets a hold on a victim with its teeth, it releases venom that quickly disables small prey. For larger animals, it may leave them to slowly die before returning to feast on them. Komodo dragons will even eat their own babies...

KILLER SCORES

DEADLY DETAILS: 8

KILLER WEAPONS: 8

ATTACK METHOD: 8

KILLER SCORE: 24/30

TOP OF THE FOOD CHAIN!

NILE CROCODILE

(Scientific name: Crocodylus niloticus)

Eats: mostly fish and reptiles but also large mammals.

4

Widespread throughout sub-Saharan Africa, the Nile crocodile is not only feared by its prey but is responsible for hundreds of human deaths every year.

DEADLY DETAILS:

Between 3.5 and 7 metres (11 and 23 ft) long, these crocs are huge and can weigh over a tonne. They have scaly hides, long jaws and powerful tails. Feared by many, they have a reputation in Africa for being man-eaters, killing over 300 people since 2008. Their muddy-bronze colouring gives them good camouflage for their watery environments.

KILLER WEAPONS:

Armed with between 64 and 68 pointed teeth in their jaws, the Nile crocodiles' main weapons include their rapid speed and agility. Coupled with more aggression than American crocodiles or alligators, this makes them a deadly opponent for any animal up to twice their size. Their bites are unimaginably strong and they can keep their grip for long periods of time.

ATTACK METHOD:

These crocs' camouflage means they can conceal themselves until the perfect moment, then they ambush their prey with a short burst of speed. They lunge their bodies out of the water, clamping their jaws around their prey and spinning in what is known as a "death roll" to drown them. Then they tear whole chunks of flesh from their catch and swallow them down in one.

KILLER SCORES

DEADLY DETAILS: 8

KILLER WEAPONS: 9

ATTACK METHOD: 9

KILLER SCORE: 26/30

POWER AND SPEED IN ONE PACKAGE

3

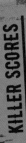

THE BLACK MAMBA

(Scientific name: *Dendroaspis polylepis*)

Eats: small birds and mammals.

KILLER SCORES

DEADLY DETAILS: 9

KILLER WEAPONS: 9

ATTACK METHOD: 10

KILLER SCORE: 28/30

CERTAIN DEATH

The black mamba is a fast, fierce and territorial snake which lives in the savannahs of southern and eastern Africa.

DEADLY DETAILS:

The name "black mamba" is deceptive – these snakes are actually brown in colour but they are named after the blue-black insides of their mouths, which they show to predators as a warning when threatened. They can grow to 4 metres (13 ft) in length, although the norm is 2.5 metres (8 ft).

KILLER WEAPONS:

The most terrifying thing about this snake is its combination of speed, aggression and deadly venom. It's the fastest-moving land snake on the planet, reaching 19 kilometres per hour (11 mph), and its venom can kill a mouse in five minutes. It has the quickest-acting venom of all snakes, which can kill a human within 20 minutes.

ATTACK METHOD:

Black mambas hiss and raise their bodies off the ground when they are ready to attack. They expose the insides of their mouths before striking quickly and repeatedly with accurate bites to the body or head. Unlike some other snakes, who sometimes bite with "dry bites" (no venom), the black mamba will inject its venom every single time.

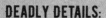

52

KING COBRA

(Scientific name: *Ophiophagus hannah*)

Eats: birds, small mammals, lizards, eggs and other snakes.

Living in various parts of Asia, the king cobra is considered the deadliest of all cobra species due to the amount of venom it injects into its prey in one go.

DEADLY DETAILS:

King cobras can grow to over 5 metres (16 ft) long. They're easily identified by their trademark hoods and their intimidating postures when they hoist themselves upright. They are excellent climbers of trees and have super-sharp eyesight and an excellent sense of smell.

KILLER WEAPONS:

Though most cobra species slither away when threatened, the king cobra is more confrontational and will stand its ground. The amount and strength of the venom it injects into its prey with one strike of its fangs is enough to kill an adult elephant or 20 people. It causes problems with vision, difficulty breathing and ultimately death – all within 30–45 minutes.

KILLER SCORES

DEADLY DETAILS: 9

KILLER WEAPONS: 9

ATTACK METHOD: 9

KILLER SCORE: 27/30

KILLER VENOM AND SUPER SPEED

ATTACK METHOD:

King cobras usually follow their prey silently until they spot the perfect moment to strike with their venomous bites. When confronted with a threat, they lift a whole third of their body weight to stand upright in a defensive display. They flare their hoods and hiss as a warning, and have the speed to dart forward from this position in the blink of an eye.

GOLDEN DART FROG

(Scientific name: Phyllobates terribilis)   Eats: small insects, like ants and termites.

1

Did you know?

Indigenous communities of Colombia use the poison from these frogs in their blowgun darts for hunting – this is where the "dart" part of their name comes from.

The golden dart frog is the most dangerous frog on Earth. It lives in the rainforests of Central and South America and produces one of the deadliest toxins in existence.

KILLER WEAPONS:

These frogs are not predators themselves but their defence strategy is one of the deadliest in the world. They produce a poison in their skin glands which is so lethal that just one frog has enough to kill 20,000 mice or 10 grown men.

DEADLY DETAILS:

These tiny frogs measure between just 1–6 centimetres (0.4–2.4 in). Their colours are bright to act as warning signs to predators – which should probably steer well clear!

ATTACK METHOD:

These frogs don't need to do anything to kill their predators except sit and wait. If their colours don't act as enough of a deterrent, a thin layer of the powerful poison sits on their skin and causes paralysis, sickness and death in minutes for anyone who touches or eats it. Even an animal who touches a spot where one of these frogs has recently been can suffer the poison's effects.

KILLER FACT

ADULT FROGS PASS POISON ONTO THEIR BABIES TO PROTECT THEM AGAINST BEING EATEN BY PREDATORS.

KILLER SCORES

DEADLY DETAILS: 9

KILLER WEAPONS: 10

ATTACK METHOD: 10

KILLER SCORE: 29/30

PRETTY BUT DEADLY

TEST YOUR KNOWLEDGE!

Now that you've read all about these killer reptiles and amphibians, see if you can answer these questions:

1. Fill in the gap:
Nile crocodiles can kill prey _____ their size.
a. three times **b.** four times **c.** twice

2. Which animal is sometimes easily mistaken for a rock?
_____
a. Alligator snapping turtle **b.** Mata mata turtle **c.** Gila monster

3. How much can a Komodo dragon weigh? _____
a. Over 50 kilograms (110 lbs) **b.** Over 100 kilograms (220 lbs)
c. Over 200 kilograms (440 lbs)

4. What is a golden dart frog's warning sign to predators?
_____
a. Its loud vocal sounds **b.** Its bright colours **c.** Its strong smell

5. A king cobra raises how much of its body off the ground when attacking? _____
a. a quarter **b.** a third **c.** half

WORD WRIGGLE

Can you fit these words into the spaces?
The first two have been done for you.

POISON   TEETH   MONSTER   PREY

BITE   VENOM   PREDATOR

Answers on page 94

KILLER
CREEPY
CRAWLIES

When you think of killer creatures, the first things to come to mind are probably some of the bigger animals on the planet. But as you'll find out over the next few pages, bigger doesn't always mean deadlier... Some of the smallest creatures in the world can cause a lot of damage. Meet some deadly arthropods – creatures without backbones – including insects, spiders and centipedes. They make up over 80 per cent of all species on Earth.

DEER TICK

(Scientific name: Ixodes scapularis)

Eats: blood from mammals such as dogs, deer and humans.

Known mostly for the deadly diseases they carry, these tiny insects are feared by people throughout the central and eastern United States.

DEADLY DETAILS:

Deer ticks have flattened bodies, eight legs and are only as big as a sesame seed. They have reddish-brown bodies and are really tricky to spot – making them all the deadlier...

ATTACK METHOD:

Deer ticks don't jump or fly, but they hang around in grassy areas ready to cling on to an animal's coat. Then they latch on and sink their mouthparts into the skin until blood flows into their bodies, refusing to let go until they've had their fill of blood!

KILLER WEAPONS:

Deer ticks might look small, but you wouldn't want to be bitten by one. Though a bite from their sharp mouthparts is painless, that's not necessarily a good thing. It can unleash Lyme disease into the bloodstreams of deer, livestock, pets or humans. It's a horrible disease that causes a rash, headaches, memory issues and potentially fatal heart and nerve problems.

KILLER SCORES

DEADLY DETAILS: 4

KILLER WEAPONS: 4

ATTACK METHOD: 7

KILLER SCORE: 15/30

TINY TICKS OF TROUBLE!

BULLET ANT

(Scientific name: *Paraponera clavata*)   Eats: nectar and other insects.

The bullet ants of South America get their name from the instant pain of their venomous sting, which is said to be comparable to being shot by a gun!

Did you know?

To prove they are ready to be warriors, boys of the Sateré-Mawe community in Brazil have to endure the pain of putting their hands into gloves filled with bullet ants, and getting stung over and over.

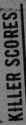

KILLER SCORES

DEADLY DETAILS: 4

KILLER WEAPONS: 7

ATTACK METHOD: 5

KILLER SCORE: 16/30

PAIN ON A GRAND SCALE

DEADLY DETAILS:

Living in groups of a few hundred to each nest, bullet ants are usually between 2–3 centimetres (0.8–1.2 in) in size – huge for an ant – with two blunt horns at the front. They look like wingless wasps but are red-black in colour.

KILLER WEAPONS:

A bit like bees, these ants will only sting humans if threatened (watch where you step!). The main purpose of their sting is to protect themselves or disable prey such as caterpillars. Their bites cause swelling, paralysis and bruising in humans and are thought to be amongst the most painful experiences known to man.

ATTACK METHOD:

They grab onto their prey or enemy with their mouths before injecting the venom. It's thought that some of the worker ants guard the nest against enemies while others go off in search of nectar from plants or insects to feed on.

KILLER FACT

THE PAIN FROM A BULLET ANT'S STING LASTS A WHOLE 24 HOURS.

REDBACK SPIDER

(Scientific name: Latrodectus hasselti)
Eats: flies and other small insects.

Redback spiders are common in Australia and are often found in garden sheds and even underneath toilet seats!

DEADLY DETAILS:

Redbacks are related to the famous black widow spider but look slightly different – redbacks have a distinctive red stripe on their rounded abdomens, which acts as a warning to other animals to stay away. Females are bigger than males and measure just 1 centimetre (0.39 in) across.

KILLER WEAPONS:

Female redbacks are much more dangerous than males. Their killer weapon is their bite, which serves to paralyse their prey by injecting it with venom so that it is ready to eat. In humans, the venom can target the nervous system, causing vomiting, fevers and severe pain for anything between hours and days. Around 2,000 people are bitten every year by redbacks.

KILLER SCORES

DEADLY DETAILS: 7

KILLER WEAPONS: 6

ATTACK METHOD: 6

KILLER SCORE: 19/30

A RED STRIPE FOR DANGER

ATTACK METHOD:

Redbacks don't hunt for their prey – they wait patiently for an unsuspecting insect to wander into their webs. Once in the web, the redback wraps its prey in silk. It bites down on the prey, injecting its venom to paralyse it. The venom also contains proteins called enzymes, which dissolve the prey's insides to make a tasty meal. These spiders will even steal wrapped-up food from other spiders' webs if they get the chance!

GIANT CENTIPEDE

7

(Scientific name: Scolopendra gigantea)

Eats: insects, spiders, rodents, birds and lizards.

These giants of the centipede world live in parts of South America and the Caribbean. They will eat anything they can overpower.

KILLER SCORES

DEADLY DETAILS: 7

KILLER WEAPONS: 6

ATTACK METHOD: 7

KILLER SCORE: 20/30

THE STUFF OF NIGHTMARES

DEADLY DETAILS:

With up to 46 legs (23 pairs) and measuring up to a jaw-dropping 35 centimetres (13 in) long, these critters send a shiver up anyone's spine who sees them skittering along a forest floor. They have two antennae on their heads for feeling around and two fangs (called mandibles) full of venom.

KILLER WEAPONS:

One heart-stopping injection of venom from the fangs of one of these is lethal for most small animals. They can run swiftly but also climb walls to catch prey. Thankfully, their poison isn't quite strong enough to kill a healthy human adult, but is enough to seriously wound – a bite from one of these causes sharp pain, swelling, muscle weakness and fever.

ATTACK METHOD:

These fierce and aggressive creatures can coil their entire bodies around their enemies or prey to help deliver their bites. They can even be found hanging upside down from cave ceilings, with just a few legs clinging on, attempting to catch bats!

LONOMIA CATERPILLAR

(Scientific name: Lonomia obliqua)   Eats: plants and tree leaves.

The lonomia caterpillar, also known as the giant silkworm moth caterpillar, causes a few human deaths every year in South America.

DEADLY DETAILS:

Lonomia caterpillars are around 5.5 centimetres (2 in) long and have dark bodies covered in long spines and hairs. Hidden away against the trees of the rainforest, these caterpillars are tricky to spot until it's too late.

KILLER WEAPONS:

Just accidentally touching one of these caterpillars can cost you your life. The fragile hairs on their skin release a toxin that can lead to so much internal bleeding that a human would eventually bleed to death. Their impressive camouflage is as much of a weapon as the toxin – helping them hide from predators.

Did you know?

Once they've transformed into moths, they become absolutely harmless!

ATTACK METHOD:

Though these caterpillars don't use their killer toxins to hunt (they prefer to feast on plants), they do use them against anything that tries to hunt *them*. Animals die trying to eat them, though most are warned by their odd appearance to stay away in the first place.

KILLER SCORES

DEADLY DETAILS: 8
KILLER WEAPONS: 8
ATTACK METHOD: 5
KILLER SCORE: 21/30
A DEADLY SHOW-STOPPER

KILLER FACT

THESE CATERPILLARS USUALLY HANG OUT IN GROUPS, SO YOU ARE MORE LIKELY TO TOUCH A FEW AT A TIME THAN JUST ONE, AND TO SUFFER THE DEADLY CONSEQUENCES...

BRAZILIAN WANDERING SPIDER

(Scientific name: Phoneutria fera)

Eats: crickets, other insects, mice and lizards.

Found in South and Central America, just the name of this spider is enough to strike fear into those who have come across one!

DEADLY DETAILS:

This is a hairy spider with red jaws and a leg span as long as 12 centimetres (4 in). It's called a "wandering" spider because it doesn't stay put in a burrow or a web, which makes it even more dangerous – it's more likely to come across the path of a human.

KILLER WEAPONS:

A bite from this spider instantly kills its prey. If it bites a human and secretes a big dose of venom, it can leave its victim paralysed or with breathing problems – leading to death within hours. But it's not just the venom in this spider's bite that should be feared – it's the pain from the bite itself. It's said to be one of the most excruciating bites of all spiders...

ATTACK METHOD:

These spiders seek out their prey instead of waiting to catch it in a web. They use their fangs to inject their target with venom and to move what they've caught into the right position for eating. When threatened, these spiders rear up on their back legs and sway from side to side, showing their red jaws as a warning ... before shooting forward to attack.

KILLER SCORES

DEADLY DETAILS: 8

KILLER WEAPONS: 7

ATTACK METHOD: 7

KILLER SCORE: 22/30

A SPIDER LOOKING FOR TROUBLE!

FAT-TAILED SCORPION

(Scientific name: Androctonus spp.)

Eats: crickets and other insects.

4

Fat-tailed scorpions are found throughout the Middle East and parts of Africa and Asia, in desert environments. They get their name from the size of their tails and are feared by people for miles around...

DEADLY DETAILS:

These scorpions grow to around 10 centimetres (4 in) long and can be a variety of colours from yellow to black. They hunt by night so during the day they hide out of sight, using their excellent camouflage. Unfortunately, they like to hide in places near to human settlements, like under wood, rubble and even inside houses.

KILLER WEAPONS:

Their hard shells are excellent defence weapons – protecting them from being eaten. But their main weapon is their tail, with a sting that can inject venom as powerful as a cobra snake's. The venom targets the nervous system, including the heart muscles, and can kill a human in minutes. Like most scorpions, they also have pincers for crushing or holding onto prey.

ATTACK METHOD:

Fat-tailed scorpions prowl for their prey at night. They'll even sneak into other animals' burrows if there's an opportunity for food. Once they've caught something with their crushing pincers, they inject their venom from their sting. Scorpions can't eat solid food so the purpose of the venom is to liquefy the prey's insides. Then it's ready for them to suck out!

KILLER SCORES

DEADLY DETAILS: 7

KILLER WEAPONS: 8

ATTACK METHOD: 8

KILLER SCORE: 23/30

PACKING A POWERFUL PUNCH

SYDNEY FUNNEL-WEB SPIDER

(Scientific name: Atrax robustus)
Eats: insects, lizards and snails.

The Sydney funnel-web spiders are named after the shape of the webs they create to catch prey. They are without a doubt the deadliest spiders in Australia, and likely the whole world.

DEADLY DETAILS:

Measuring 1–5 centimetres (0.4–2 in) long, these spiders are glossy black-brown, with large pincers and legs measuring up to 8 centimetres (3 in) long. They live in burrows in the ground and are known to be very bad-tempered spiders.

KILLER WEAPONS:

These are clever spiders, making little "trip wires" of silk at the entrance of their burrows for detecting any unsuspecting prey passing by. Their huge fangs can pierce through toenails and clothing, leaving obvious marks behind. They're responsible for some of the most painful and serious human bites, with the potential to cause death within 15 minutes.

KILLER SCORES

DEADLY DETAILS: 7

KILLER WEAPONS: 8

ATTACK METHOD: 10

KILLER SCORE: 25/30

CLEVER WEB DESIGNS AND A TERRIFYING BITE

ATTACK METHOD:

These spiders spend most of their time in their burrows, waiting for prey to "trip" their clever silk webs at the entrance, so that they can race out and catch it. A quick injection of venom subdues the prey enough for eating. If threatened, they rear up on their hind legs and attack again and again with their fangs, injecting venom and clinging on with a tight grip – these spiders are relentless!

SIAFU ANTS

(Scientific name: Dorylus spp.)

Eats: crickets and other insects.

Truly terrifying creatures, these African ants are a perfect example of strength in numbers. They are also known as "driver ants" or "safari ants".

KILLER SCORES

DEADLY DETAILS: 8

KILLER WEAPONS: 9

ATTACK METHOD: 10

KILLER SCORE: 27/30

THE ULTIMATE FEAR FACTOR

DEADLY DETAILS:

They might be small, but they travel in enormous colonies! A colony can have over 20 million ants, all marching together along the floor. They move from place to place, consuming their food supply until there's nothing left, before moving on.

KILLER WEAPONS:

Perhaps the scariest thing about these ants is that they're clever. They travel with attack ants either side of the colony to defend the workers on the inside lines. They behave as if they're one big being – if one ant is stepped on, the whole colony will swarm and attack. Their cutting bites are incredibly powerful and it's difficult to pull these ants off once they're attached.

2

ATTACK METHOD:

Another thing that makes these ants so scary is that they don't eat vegetation – they eat meat! And they'll try to attack anything that gets in their way. That includes injured or weak mammals ... even humans. One small comfort is that they don't actually eat large creatures alive – they're more likely to overwhelm and suffocate them.

DEATHSTALKER SCORPION

(Scientific name: Leiurus quinquestriatus)　Eats: worms, centipedes, crickets and other insects.

The Palestine scorpion is the deadliest scorpion in the world and has earned the nickname "Deathstalker" from people living in its native habitat of North Africa and the Middle East.

1

Did you know?

The deathstalker's venom has proven to be useful in medicine – showing potential for treating cancer tumours and diabetes.

KILLER SCORES

DEADLY DETAILS: 10

KILLER WEAPONS: 10

ATTACK METHOD: 9

KILLER SCORE: 29/30

LIVING UP TO ITS NAME!

DEADLY DETAILS:

Between 3–8 centimetres (1–3 in) long, this scorpion might be small but it is definitely deadly enough to make it to number one in this countdown! It has two large pincers and a lethal sting at the end of its tail. Its yellow colour helps it hide in the desert sand, ready to strike at passing prey or any humans who accidentally disturb it...

KILLER WEAPONS:

Its stinger is known as a telson and is used in defence or to paralyse prey. It has sacs of venom and a sharp barb that injects the venom into the scorpion's target. While most scorpions are relatively harmless to humans, this is a particularly dangerous species due to the power of its venom. If you're unlucky enough to be stung by one of these, it can cause unbearable pain, paralysis and death. Its pincers are also razor sharp and are used to tear apart prey for eating.

ATTACK METHOD:

Just like the name suggests, these scorpions take their prey by surprise after stalking them. They grab their prey with their pincers, but as they're not that strong, they go straight in with a sting, jabbing the prey repeatedly. This disables the prey enough to be torn apart for a delicious meal.

KILLER FACT

JUST ONE TINY DROP OF THE DEATHSTALKER'S VENOM CAN KILL AROUND 40 MICE!

TEST YOUR KNOWLEDGE!

Now that you've read all about these killer creepy crawlies, see if you can answer these questions:

1. Where can you find siafu ants?_____

2. Which creature is known to steal food from spider webs?

_____

3. What is another name for the Palestine scorpion?

_____

4. The fat-tailed scorpion can't eat _____ food.

5. Which spider doesn't make a web?_____

6. A colony of siafu ants can include over _____ ants.

7. How long does the pain from a bullet ant's sting last?

_____

8. How many pairs of legs can a giant centipede have?

_____

Can you fit these words into the spaces?
The first two have been done for you.

~~DISEASE~~   STINGER   PINCERS   FANGS

~~BITE~~   DEADLY   SPIDER

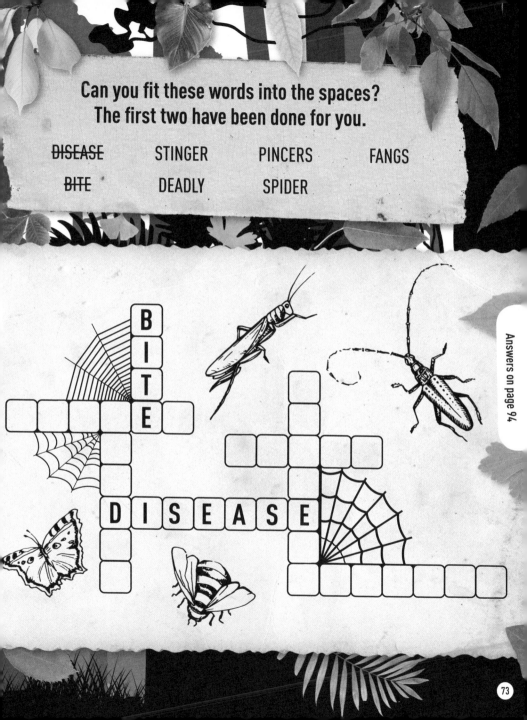

Answers on page 94

KILLER
WINGED
CREATURES

Ranging in size from giant birds to tiny insects, the following animals all have one thing in common – they have wings! Wings don't always mean flight – there are many creatures with wings who never take to the sky. But wings still give these animals that little something extra – whether used as weapons, for extra mobility or sometimes, it seems, just to terrify us...

GREAT HORNED OWL

(Scientific name: Bubo virginianus)
Eats: rodents, squirrels, birds and fish.

10

The most common owl of the Americas, the great horned owl is named after the feather tufts on its head, which resemble horns.

DEADLY DETAILS:

These owls can be 50 centimetres (19 in) tall with wingspans of 1.5 metres (4 ft). Their colours change depending on where they live, but they all have the distinctive tufts of feathers on their heads. Like most owls, their eyes face forwards but they can rotate their necks 270 degrees to see in all directions.

KILLER WEAPONS:

They use their excellent eyesight and sense of hearing to find their prey, making use of their camouflage to hide out of sight and watch from above. Though they have no teeth, they have sharp beaks for stripping flesh and pointed talons for striking and grabbing prey up to three times their own size.

ATTACK METHOD:

Great horned owls glide silently above the ground until they spot potential food. Then they fold their wings and swoop without warning at 60 kilometres per hour (37 mph), seizing the prey with their curved talons. The prey is often killed instantly and the owls are able to swallow it whole. They're fiercely protective of their young and have been known to also attack humans who get too close.

KILLER SCORES

DEADLY DETAILS: 4
KILLER WEAPONS: 6
ATTACK METHOD: 7
KILLER SCORE: 17/30
TOP-NOTCH PREDATORS

AFRICAN OSTRICH

(Scientific name: Struthio camelus)

Eats: plants, seeds, insects and lizards.

9

The African ostrich is the largest bird on Earth. Though flightless, they have strong weapons for defending themselves and their territories...

KILLER WEAPONS:

They have long, massive leg bones and just two toes on each foot, to help them run faster. They can reach speeds of 70 kilometres per hour (43 mph) so can outrun any other animal with their 3 metre (9 ft) long strides. Each foot also has a sharp claw and the ostrich is armed with a perilously strong downward kick.

DEADLY DETAILS:

Ostriches have black and white plumage with elongated necks and large eyes and eyelashes, which make them look almost comical.
But these birds aren't to be laughed at – at 145 kilograms (319 lb) and 2.5 metres (8 ft) tall, these are the giants of the bird world!

KILLER SCORES

DEADLY DETAILS: 7
KILLER WEAPONS: 5
ATTACK METHOD: 6
KILLER SCORE: 18/30
GIANTS OF THE BIRD WORLD

ATTACK METHOD:

When startled, ostriches will usually run away or flatten themselves to the ground in an attempt to become less visible. Their feathers blend in with the ground around them so they look as if they have buried their heads in the sand. If threatened, they fight with their feet, kicking forward with enough force to kill a lion.

Living in the rainforests of north-western Australia and New Guinea, the southern cassowary is the world's most dangerous bird...

8

SOUTHERN CASSOWARY

(Scientific name: Casuarius casuarius)
Eats: small mammals, insects, fruit.

DEADLY DETAILS:

With black feathers, patches of blue skin and a bony head, these flightless giant birds look a bit like dinosaurs. They stand at nearly 1.8 metres (6 ft) tall (as tall as an adult man) and can weigh around 60 kilograms (132 lb).

KILLER WEAPONS:

Although they mainly forage for fruit, these birds are fiercely territorial. They have powerful legs, long feet and three sharp claws with a dagger-like middle one that reaches 12 centimetres (4 in) in length. They are also able to jump up to 1 metre (39 in) in the air. Despite not being as big or as fast as ostriches, cassowaries have more of a reputation for being aggressive towards humans.

ATTACK METHOD:

When startled, cassowaries will usually run – at a speed of 50 kilometres per hour (31 mph). But if cornered or if they need to protect their young, these birds can jump and kick with both legs at once. Their strong legs and slicing claws are powerful enough to rip open another animal. Once provoked, they will keep chasing and attacking their victim.

KILLER SCORES

DEADLY DETAILS: 6

KILLER WEAPONS: 6

ATTACK METHOD: 7

KILLER SCORE: 19/30

NINJA BIRDS

TSETSE FLY

(Scientific name: Glossina spp)
Eats: blood.

Packing a painful bite, these blood-sucking monsters of the insect world are known for spreading a dangerous parasitic disease throughout sub-Saharan Africa...

KILLER FACT

SLEEPING SICKNESS CAUSES AROUND 10,000 HUMAN DEATHS EVERY YEAR.

Did you know?

Even the larvae of the tsetse fly are dangerous – they produce a toxin that is strong enough to kill a human!

DEADLY DETAILS:

At just 8–17 millimetres (0.3–0.7 in) long – the same size as a house fly – you wouldn't think these flies were able to do much damage. They look similar in shape to a common housefly, too, but one thing makes them unique: they survive by feeding off the blood of other animals...

KILLER WEAPONS:

They might not look deadly, but when a tsetse fly feasts on the blood of an animal or human, using its long, piercing proboscis, it can infect the animal with parasites called trypanosomes. These are shaped like eels and can cause a disease known as African sleeping sickness where the victim suffers from fevers, damage to the nervous system and even death.

ATTACK METHOD:

A tsetse fly's bite is extremely painful and hard to ignore. Once bitten, the parasites can spread from the fly through the victim's bloodstream and into the nervous system, causing the sickness. Cows are often affected, meaning that farmers in Africa lose livestock to the disease. Whole livelihoods are put at risk by these flies.

KILLER SCORES

DEADLY DETAILS: 5

KILLER WEAPONS: 9

ATTACK METHOD: 6

KILLER SCORE: 20/30

SNEAKY AND DEADLY

COMMON VAMPIRE BAT

(Scientific name: *Desmodus rotundus*)

Eats: the blood of mammals like tapirs and horses.

6

Vampire bats have fearsome reputations as South American mammals that feed on the blood of other animals.

DEADLY DETAILS:

These aren't just the stuff of legends – these blood-sucking creatures are very real! They have dark, greyish-brown coats and wingspans of around 40 centimetres (15 in). The bats live in colonies of around 100 animals, which can drink the blood of 25 cows between them in just one year.

KILLER WEAPONS:

Bats are the only mammals that can fly. They use their ears to "see" by making high-pitched noises and listening for the echoes. The information they get from these echoes helps them to work out where their prey is. Vampire bats also have heat sensors to detect where the warm blood is beneath the skin, with scalpel-like teeth to get to it and specially grooved lips for lapping it up.

ATTACK METHOD:

Cattle and horses are these bats' usual targets, which they attack from the ground, though they have been known to attack humans as well. First they bite, then lap up the blood that flows from the wound. They drink the blood of their victims for about 30 minutes at a time, using a saliva that stops it from clotting until the bats have consumed about half their own body weight in blood.

KILLER SCORES

DEADLY DETAILS: 7

KILLER WEAPONS: 6

ATTACK METHOD: 7

KILLER SCORE: 20/30

HALLOWEEN HORRORS

AFRICANISED HONEY BEE

(Scientific name: Apis mellifera scutelatta)
Eats: pollen and honey made from nectar.

Causing around 40 deaths in the United States every year, these insects aren't known as "killer bees" for nothing!

5

DEADLY DETAILS:

Africanised honey bees look just like other honey bee species – with their two wings, antennae and segmented bodies – but are slightly smaller than their European relatives. They make homes in the eaves of houses, in trees and small sheltered places like old car tyres.

KILLER WEAPONS:

These bees are sensitive to the presence of humans and much more aggressive than other bee species when they feel threatened. The venom they inject with each sting isn't too strong by itself, but enough of it all at once can kill a large mammal... So the fact that these bees tend to attack in huge swarms makes them extremely lethal.

ATTACK METHOD:

Usually collecting pollen as a food source, these bees will only attack to defend their hives. But when they do attack, thousands can surround the victim at a time, flying into eyes and ears and swarming and stinging again and again. The only way to escape is to keep running...

PEREGRINE FALCON

(Scientific name: Falco peregrinus)

Eats: other birds and bats.

Peregrine falcons can dive at speeds that make them the fastest animals in the whole world. They live on every continent except for Antarctica.

DEADLY DETAILS:

Peregrines are large and powerful birds, with wingspans of up to 1.1 metres (3 ft 7 in). They have short tails, blue-grey heads and white, speckled bodies. Their name means "wanderer", which is fitting for a bird that can be found all over the world, from shorelines to skyscrapers.

KILLER WEAPONS:

Peregrines are adapted to be fast and efficient predators. Their lightweight bones make them swift and agile and they have special cones in their noses to help them breathe when they're diving quickly. They also have hooked beaks and strong talons for catching and tearing at prey.

ATTACK METHOD:

From the air, peregrines search open spaces for prey, but rarely target ground-dwelling animals. Instead, they chase their prey through the sky in an attempt to catch it mid-flight or dive for it from a great height. They strike it with their feet to stun or kill it, then twist around to catch it mid-air in a dazzling aerial display.

Did you know?

Peregrines reach speeds of 322 kilometres per hour (200 mph) when they dive, making them the fastest animals on Earth.

KILLER SCORES

DEADLY DETAILS: 6

KILLER WEAPONS: 8

ATTACK METHOD: 10

KILLER SCORE: 24/30

PREDATOR OF THE SKIES

KILLER FACT

THEIR BEAKS ARE ADAPTED FOR SEVERING THE SPINAL COLUMNS OF THEIR PREY AT THE NECK.

ASSASSIN BUG

(Scientific name: Rhodnius prolixus)

Eats: blood from animals like rats, opossums, dogs and humans.

3

This species of assassin bug from the United States is sometimes called the "kissing bug" due to its reputation for biting humans and other mammals around the lips!

DEADLY DETAILS:

Dark brown or black, with orange markings, these bugs measure around 3 centimetres (1.3 in) at their largest. They have six long legs and folded wings, although they don't fly very frequently.

KILLER WEAPONS:

These bugs have piercing beaks designed to suck blood from their victims, and a single tube that transfers their poisonous saliva, which liquefies the insides. This species can infect any victim it bites with a deadly disease called trypanosomiasis, or Chagas disease, which causes fevers, fatigue, vomiting and death for around 10,000 people every year.

ATTACK METHOD:

These bugs either stalk their prey or wait for something tasty to walk by, before suddenly attacking with their beaks and sucking out their victim's insides. They hunt at night, and also attack animals like humans and dogs when they're sleeping. When they bite, they poo at the same time, before rubbing their faeces into the bite wound! This is how Chagas is transmitted.

KILLER SCORES

DEADLY DETAILS: 7

KILLER WEAPONS: 8

ATTACK METHOD: 10

KILLER SCORE: 25/30

A GRUESOME ENDING

GIANT JAPANESE HORNET

(Scientific name: Vespa mandarinia japonica)

Eats: larger insects like mantises and honey from honey bees.

2

The giant Japanese hornet is the world's largest hornet and an excellent predator of other insects, including honey bees.

DEADLY DETAILS:

Up to 4.5 centimetres (1 in) in length and with wingspans of more than 6 centimetres (2 in) – bigger than a hummingbird's – these are enormous flying killing machines! They're about as big as an adult human's thumb and have large, yellow heads with brown-and-yellow bodies.

KILLER WEAPONS:

Heavily armoured, with strong mouthparts and stingers that are half a centimetre long, you wouldn't want to be on the wrong side of one of these ... Apart from being as painful as a hot nail in your skin, their sting injects venom that can cause an allergic reaction in people, leading to a number of deaths in Japan every year. They're also fast – travelling at 40 kilometres per hour (24 mph).

ATTACK METHOD:

These hornets are especially known for wiping out colonies of honey bees, devouring tens of thousands of bees a day. Five times the size of the bees, they use their mouthparts – or mandibles – to strip off the bees' wings and legs, dragging their nutritious bodies to their nests. They chew the bodies to make a paste and feed it to their larvae, before feasting on the fluid their larvae produce.

KILLER SCORES

DEADLY DETAILS: 8

KILLER WEAPONS: 8

ATTACK METHOD: 9

KILLER SCORE: 25/30

WIPING OUT ALL COMPETITION

ANOPHELES MOSQUITO

(Scientific name: Anopheles spp)

Eats: blood, nectar and fruit.

Anopheles mosquitoes kill more people than any other animal on the planet. They're found all over the world, except Antarctica.

Did you know?

Only the females of this species of mosquito bite humans. They need the blood to nurture their eggs whereas males are happy to feast on nectar.

KILLER FACT

MALARIA IS RESPONSIBLE FOR THE DEATH OF ALMOST A MILLION PEOPLE EVERY YEAR.

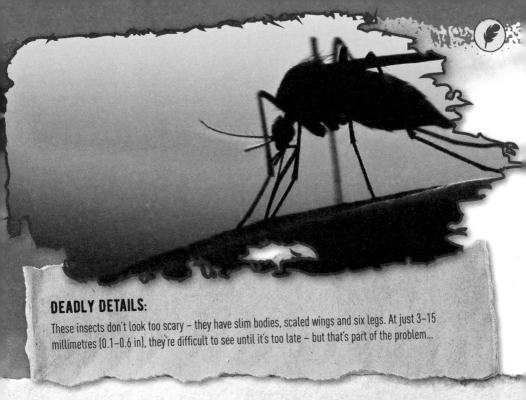

DEADLY DETAILS:

These insects don't look too scary – they have slim bodies, scaled wings and six legs. At just 3–15 millimetres (0.1–0.6 in), they're difficult to see until it's too late – but that's part of the problem...

KILLER WEAPONS:

Mosquitoes drink blood using their long proboscises, which are two feeding tubes shaped like needles. That alone isn't usually much of a problem, but some females of this mosquito species can infect their hosts with the deadly malaria virus. Some other species of mosquitoes can also kill by themselves – in the Arctic, swarms of millions of mosquitoes have been known to kill by draining caribou of their blood!

ATTACK METHOD:

Mosquitoes are easy to squash or bat away, but aren't usually noticed until they've already done their damage. When they bite with their needle-like proboscis, the saliva they inject into the skin includes something called "histamines", which irritate the skin and cause itching. But by then, any disease will have already made its way into the victim's bloodstream...

KILLER SCORES

DEADLY DETAILS: 9

KILLER WEAPONS: 10

ATTACK METHOD: 10

KILLER SCORE: 29/30
THE MOST DANGEROUS ANIMAL ON EARTH

TRUE OR FALSE?

Can you guess whether the statements below are true or false?

		TRUE	FALSE
1.	Ostriches don't have teeth so they swallow pebbles to help grind their food.		
2.	Tsetse flies are attracted to bright colours.		
3.	If a mosquito drinks more than its body weight in blood it can explode.		
4.	Peregrine falcons pluck any feathers from their prey before eating it.		
5.	A killer bee releases chemicals that smell like bananas to attract other members of its colony to its location.		
6.	Great horned owls hunt during the day so that they can easily spot their prey.		
7.	Ostriches have the largest eyes of any land animal.		
8.	Japanese people eat giant hornets.		

SPOT THE DIFFERENCE

Can you spot the FIVE differences between these pictures?

Answers on page 94

G B E X U P R S T I N G
J K E Y Z C W E N S G J
A F D A H N B L O O D G
A W V T K F L V R D H K
Q I E T Y I S O I P L J
P N N B C Z P A S A F H
M G V R E D E A X R H T
L S H E R O E R H A T A
H N D G K J D J A S F L
R W A X H Q G V E I H O
G M A L A R I A T T E N
B X L R J K W S Y E M E

Can you find these words hidden in the grid above?

WINGS • TALON • BEAK • BLOOD
PARASITE • SPEED • MALARIA • STING

MATCH THE FACTS

Can you draw a line to match the statement to the animal?

A. The only mammals that can fly •

B. A big threat to honey bees •

C. Can kill a lion with a kick •

D. Responsible for around a million human deaths every year •

E. Can swallow its prey whole •

F. Fastest animal on Earth •

Answers on page 94

ACTIVITY ANSWERS

PAGE 20

PAGE 21

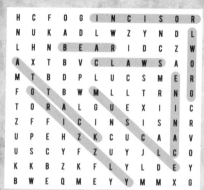

PAGE 22

CLAWS (vertical)

SPEED

POWE (vertical, POWER)

TERRITORY

STEALTH

ATTACK (vertical)

HUNT (vertical)

PAGE 23

1. FALSE –
they live in the
African savannah

2. TRUE

3. TRUE

4. FALSE –
they have 36!

5. FALSE –
they remain active
all year round

6. TRUE

7. TRUE

8. FALSE –
but they are scared
of ants and bees!

ACTIVITY ANSWERS

PAGE 38

PAGE 39

1. TRUE
2. TRUE
3. TRUE
4. FALSE – they are scavengers
5. TRUE
6. FALSE – but it's still an incredible figure – 45,000!
7. TRUE (only half of their brains ever go to sleep at a time)
8. FALSE – they can smell a single drop of blood in 200 litres (that's over 350 pint glasses) of water!

PAGE 41

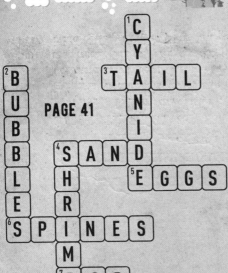

PAGE 56

1. c
2. a
3. b
4. b
5. b

PAGE 72

1. Africa
2. Redback spider
3. Deathstalker
4. Solid
5. Brazilian wandering spider
6. 20 million
7. 24 hours
8. 23

ACTIVITY ANSWERS

PAGE 57

```
    B
P O I S O N
    I
    T   V E N O M
    E           O
            T   N
            E   S   P
P R E D A T O R   R
            T   E   E
            H   R   Y
```

PAGE 73

```
        B
        I
  S P I D E R         P
        E       F A N G S
        A             I
        D I S E A S E C
        L             E
        Y             R
                      S T I N G E R
```

PAGE 89

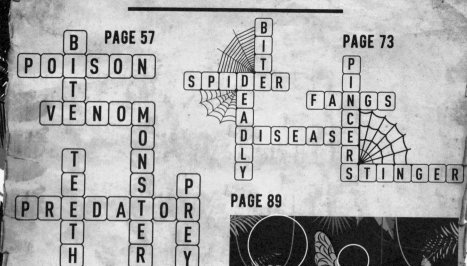

PAGE 88

1. TRUE
2. FALSE – they're attracted to dark colours
3. FALSE – they can drink up to three times their own body weight in blood
4. TRUE
5. TRUE
6. FALSE – they are nocturnal animals
7. TRUE
8. TRUE

PAGE 90

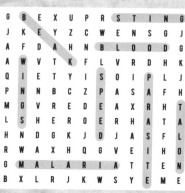

PAGE 91

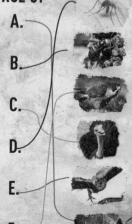

A.
B.
C.
D.
E.
F.